Horse Training

Acquire Proficiency In Comprehending, Instructing, And Interacting With Your Equine Companion Within A Span Of 30 Days Through The Implementation Of Groundwork, Equine Psychology, Saddle Training, And The Initiation Of Young Horses

Cornelius Lohse

TABLE OF CONTENT

Outfitting The Booth 1

Unhealthy Horse Behaviours 9

Heavy Horse Breakdown 36

Increasing Suppleness Even Further 54

How To Take Charge Of Your Equine 82

Analysing The Information From The Interview . 103

Outfitting The Booth

The furniture in a stall or shelter is minimal. They can be painful for your horse's feet and are typically made of gravel and hard-packed soil. Stall mats can be used to offer one inch of cushioning to the shelter. Rubber stall mats typically measure four by six feet. Six mats can cover the majority of shelter flooring. To prevent the majority of the hay from heaping up on the ground, the shelter should also feature a hay rack. Hay stored in a rack may get disorganised by certain horses. Those horses could need hay bags to cut down on the quantity of hay that ends up on the ground. There will be less hay on the floor thanks to the net-like bag. They will only consume the hay from the ground if it is muddy, damp, covered with manure, or has poop on it. Hay needs to be thrown out once it becomes soiled. Hay can be recycled to some extent by filling puddles and muddy areas. Some horses will squander less hay if they are in hay bags. Having a grain feeder is also beneficial to prevent food waste. You should set up the grain feeder and hay rack so your horse may be fed without having to go into his stall every time. The same holds if hay bags are being used. The hay bag in the stall can be hung using a hook that clips onto a ring that is placed directly inside the door. It is a good idea for two horses in connected paddocks to share a clean, freshwater horse trough. If a windstorm removes some shingles or the paint begins to peel, the horse shelters can require some maintenance. Some horses enjoy playing in their stalls with a big inflatable ball that is hung on a rope. Every horse in the shelter needs a salt lick. That is the scope of your shelter or stall's furnishing.

Start Your Partnership Now!

As was previously said, the goal of every interaction and activity you have with your Arab is to strengthen your bond. Speak to your Arab frequently during all interactions and activities. Share with him your opinions and remarks regarding each interaction. Give him a daily neck hug that lasts for at least 30 seconds. Smell him when you bury your face in his neck. Put your chest up against his. When you do this for the first time, he could be a little taken aback. The first few times, he could even try to move away from you. When he takes a step back, hold on. Join him as you move ahead and hang on for thirty seconds. Before time, your Arab will start to appreciate your embrace as well. As you converse with him as needed, give him instructions. Say "Walk" as soon as you put on his halter and begin leading him out of his stall, and make sure he follows you out the door. Say "Stand" as you attach him to the hitching rail and praise him each time he follows instructions.

Appropriate Management

When handling your Arab, the most important thing is keeping you safe. I'll say it again: before following these book instructions, you will need to take a few lessons if you are not familiar with handling and riding horses. Perhaps you'll need to learn how to put on a saddle, bridle, and halter. You must learn how to lift each hoof and properly clean its bottom with a hoof pick. Every day that you deal with your horse, you must be able to lead him out of the stable using a halter. You must exercise caution when working with your Arab. When a dog approaches and startles your Arab, he can respond violently. To defend himself, he can try to kick, run, or even rear up. You run the risk of being kicked, stomped, or dragged if you are not alert and prepared. After being startled, an Arab may inadvertently kill a human being. You might have to move aside or perhaps let go of his lead line in order to keep yourself safe in order to prevent such a situation. It is helpful to speak to your Arab frequently in a calming, tranquil tone. This will lessen the amount of violence your Arab will react to a shock.

Your Arab will become less easily shocked by a variety of stimuli. He'll likely adjust to having a dog. He might be surprised if you have to pass a herd of llamas while following a track because he has never seen that kind of animal before. Every time he exhales, he can snort loudly and freeze for ten seconds. Just stroke his neck and talk to him quietly. Assure him that they won't ever hurt him. As you gently walk by, tell him he's a nice boy and give him a gentle leg squeeze. After passing the llamas three times, he probably won't react any more. Talking to your Arab all the time will help in the beginning, as it will always be calming. If you speak to your Arab all the time to calm his worries, he will face and conquer most of them really quickly.

Unhealthy Horse Behaviours

Not biting

The majority of horses might try to mouth-nibble you. This could be a loving gesture with no malicious intent. If he refrains from using his teeth, it is more akin to a kiss, lick, or taste. The horse may attempt to bite you, so proceed with caution. This could occur early on, before you and your Arab have developed a trusting relationship and before your Arab has fully fallen in love. That is less of an issue after that. You must prevent any biting from occurring at first. Your aim should be to avoid ever being bitten or injured by your Arab in any way. Your Arab won't even TRY to hurt you after he's fallen in love with you.

Take it easy on the nibbles.

You might see your Arab and his pasture companion standing side by side and facing different directions if they grow close. Then you see them biting each other on the backs as they groom each other. You would be harmed if your Arab attempted to do it with you. It's probably safer to divert your Arab's attention from biting you at first. As your bond deepens, you might determine that a few kisses and nibbles are acceptable because of your trust. However, always go it easy on the nibbles, as your Arab may unintentionally bite you. I have witnessed the aftermath of horse bites, which typically include bleeding and/or bruises. Horses can be vicious animals!

Not kicking

Your Arabian horse may kick you, causing serious head injuries, bruising, broken ribs and other bones, or even worse. A kick may be accidental or purposeful. The deliberate kicks will usually happen in the early stages of your relationship; if your connection is developing slowly, it may take up to a year. An unintentional kick is more likely after that. Your Arab is unlikely to intentionally kick you if you don't put yourself in a situation where you could get kicked within the first year. You will know to exercise extra caution when dogs or other horses are around if you find out that your Arab kicks at them.

You will be aware that the dreaded unintentional kick might happen if a dog or another horse is in the area. This might happen when your Arab unintentionally kicks you when he thinks he is trying to kick the dog or horse. These inadvertent kicks have the potential to be just as harmful as deliberate ones. If you are aware that your Arab will kick at a wasp, horsefly, or bee, you should exercise the same caution if you see an annoying insect near your Arab.

Should you be aware that your Arab might attempt to kick someone, advise them to avoid approaching the Arab from the side or in front of them, and treat your Arab with the same vigilance? Be cautious around anything else your Arab might try to kick but might unintentionally kick you. You will frequently notice in the marketing that this horse does not bite or kick when you are searching to buy your new Arab. That's a good place to start. It may also state "easy keeper" in the advertisement. They don't need as much hay as other horses because they are easy keepers. It might also say "husband safe," which could refer to either one of two things: either the horse is friendly to both men and women, or a novice can ride it. All of these are crucial things to think about.

To make sure the horse is a good fit, you can request a free care lease or a three-month free trial if you are unsure about the horse for sale. These let you give the Arab a test ride so you may decide if you want to make this horse your greatest friend before committing to it. You can start looking for another horse and return the horse to its original owner if it doesn't work out. It is very advised to do this.

Don't Step on Your Toes

Allowing your Arab to tread on your foot increases the risk of fractures and/or bruises. This is another incident that might have been planned or unintentional. The deliberate stepping will only take place in the early stages of your partnership; for a slow-building relationship, this could take up to a year. An unintentional step is more likely after that. Your Arab is unlikely to intentionally walk on your feet if you don't place yourself in a position to be stepped on during the first year. Your Arab may walk on your feet on purpose or by accident when you give him a daily embrace. It's simple to embrace your Arabian while protecting your feet. Give his hooves some room between you and them. You should modify your feet if your Arab moves throughout the hug. Use the same caution whenever your feet are in front of or behind his hooves.

Don't touch its face with your body.

This is more correctly described as your Arab having an itchy face and wanting to use you as a scratching post. It is not often interpreted as an aggressive gesture. This could even be seen as a gesture of love, but when your Arab rubs his face against you, he might injure you or even knock you down. When you see your Arab coming to rub his face on you, it's a good idea to back up and let him use your hands as a scratching post. He'll soon discover that this is a productive substitute for getting his itchy spot treated. You will be safe, and your Arab will be satisfied with this.

Not pursuing

It is advisable to take your Arab outside before he is turned out in his pasture for the day after you have allowed him a few days to adjust to his new environment and put on his halter. Catching your Arab from within the paddock is far simpler than from outside the pasture. You might find that your Arab does not want to accompany you if you decide to take him out after he has already entered the meadow. He hasn't gotten to know you yet. As you approach him, he can flee from you. Never try to catch your Arab by chasing him around the meadow. Do not even try to pursue him. If he flees from you, turn around and head to grab a bucket of grain. Once more, approach him while using the bucket as bait. Whenever grain was presented to an Arab, he would frequently approach you to take a piece of it. Put a halter on him just after he enters the pasture if he still does not come. With time, your Arab will always come to you when he hears you calling his name, whistling, or holding a reward. However, never pursue an Arab.

No Retreating

When you first start dating an Arab, he can want to run away or flee from you. As was already indicated, this is another no-no: if your Arab runs away from you, do not pursue him. If there is another horse nearby that will come to you, your Arab is probably going to follow shortly after he notices the other horse getting some grain or treats. Put a halter on him just after he enters the pasture if he still does not come. With time, your Arab will never flee and will always come running to you from the pasture when you call his name, give him a treat, or whistle.

Examining Your Arabian Vet

Before committing to a new horse, I will always get it checked out by a veterinarian. I usually won't get another checkup for another one to four years or until I start to notice any health issues. I want the veterinarian to weigh and examine his eyes, teeth, and hooves every time they visit. To maintain your

Arab's health throughout their life, general care requirements must be met in addition to appropriate feeding and exercise. These consist of regular veterinarian care for teeth, feet, and immunisations; regular grooming and weatherproofing; and management of parasites. A reputable veterinarian will recommend foods and drugs for treatment. Elderly horses (those over 20 years of age) should see their veterinarian at least twice a year, if not more regularly, as sickness is more common and easier to diagnose in older animals.

Your horse's doctor can suggest a wellness programme that includes frequent blood testing. I have owned my three Arabs and cross-bred Arabs for ten years, and they are all over twenty years old. My closest friends treat my stables more like a retirement community! Right now, only one of the three can be ridden, but I want to give them the best possible life. These are happy horses living in a tiny heaven. They are fortunate.

Illnesses in Your Arab

Although numerous things can happen even before the age of 20, the majority of health issues will manifest beyond that age. There are four recognised genetic disorders in Arabian horses, and they typically cause the diseased animal to die or be put to sleep.

A test is available for severe combined immunodeficiency disorder (SCID).

Cerebellar Abiotrophy (CA) (offered as an indirect marker test)

Syndrome of Lavender Foals (LFS) (test available)

Malformation of the occipital atlantoaxial (OAAM) (test not yet available)

Tests are currently unavailable for two other conditions: juvenile epilepsy syndrome (JES) and guttural pouch tympany (GPT), the latter of which can affect dogs of different breeds.

Additional requirements for Arabs
tetanus

Constriction (Distemper)

Influenza

Pneumonia in the nose

Encephalomyelitis in Horses

rabies

Worms in the stomach

Colic

Laminitis

Sadly, there are a lot more health issues that can arise from accidents or injuries.

If you experience any symptoms, your veterinarian will also check for these illnesses. When a horse is suffering every day and has little possibility of rehabilitation, many Arab owners will make the difficult decision to put it to sleep. Your Arab is unable to make this choice on his own; it is a choice of love. Sometimes, a veterinarian may tell you that you have a 10% chance of making a full recovery if you can afford to pay $5,000 for treatment and a hospital stay. A 10% possibility does not come with a lot of money for certain Arab owners. You might never have any health issues until far into your 20s if you buy an Arab who is 5-6 years old and in excellent health. It's typical to ride your horse until he's over thirty years old or older.

You might decide to cover your horse with a blanket on chilly evenings if you live somewhere where the temperature falls into the 20s and 30s. Do you think it would feel better to have your Arab wearing a coat, and does he grow a very long winter coat? In any case, an Arab will benefit from a nighttime blanket to be warm and dry.

The winter water trough for your Arab is another thing to think about. A plug-in heater that may be placed in the trough for the winter is available at many stables. The water will never freeze if you use a plug-in heater. Your Arab will probably stick his nose through the ice to get water during the night if there is no electricity. If water is available during the freeze, you can remove the ice in the morning and replenish the trough. During the colder months, controlling the ice and flowing water can prove challenging.

Activities that Stimulate the Mind

A big inflated ball that occasionally has markings similar to a football is used for play by certain horses, or they are taught how to play with one. Your Arab may play with it independently if you buy one and place it in his paddock. If he doesn't seem interested, you can incorporate it into his round pen training later on, and who knows? He might grow intrigued. In his stall, you can also hang a ball for playtime.

Arabs can be utilised for a variety of equestrian pursuits, including contests, if preferred. Arabs are frequently utilised in endurance competitions because of their reputation for endurance. The majority of races are 50 or 100 miles long. Arab and winning cyclists can finish 100 miles in 14–15 hours. That indicates a travel speed of more than seven miles per hour on average. Although horses of any breed can compete, Arabian horses typically win at the highest levels due to their innate endurance and stamina. Although Arab horses are preferred by some riders for barrel racing, Quarter Horses are more frequently used in rodeo competitions. Although other breeds are usually used in hunter/jumper contests, some riders opt to enter an Arab.

Arabs are frequently regarded as the most beautiful horse in the competition and make good show horses. Arabian horses are willing to carry you many miles in a single day and make great trail horses. Even though you have a 16-hour workday in the summer, your Arab will take you for the entire day if you so desire. Later in this book, we'll cover more about other cognitively stimulating activities.

Outfitting the booth

The furniture in a stall or shelter is minimal. They can be painful for your Friesian horse's hooves and are typically made of gravel and hard-packed dirt. Stall mats can be used to offer one inch of cushioning to the shelter. Rubber stall mats typically measure four by six feet. Six mats can cover the majority of shelter flooring. To prevent the majority of the hay from heaping up on the ground, the shelter should also feature a hay rack.

Hay stored in a rack may get tangled by certain Friesian horses. Those horses could need hay bags to cut down on the quantity of hay that ends up on the ground. There will be less hay on the floor thanks to the net-like bag. They will only consume the hay from the ground if it is muddy, damp, covered with manure, or has poop on it. Hay needs to be thrown out once it becomes soiled. Hay can be recycled to some extent by filling puddles and muddy areas. Some horses will squander less hay if they are in hay bags.

Having a grain feeder is also beneficial to prevent food waste. It is best to arrange the grain feeder and hay rack, so your Friesian horse can be fed without having to go inside his stall every time. The same holds if hay bags are being used. The hay bag in the stall can be hung using a hook that clips onto a ring that is placed directly inside the door. It is a good idea for two horses in connected paddocks to share a clean, freshwater horse trough. If a windstorm removes some shingles or the paint begins to peel, the horse shelters can require some maintenance. In their stall, several Friesian horses like playing with a big inflated ball that is hung on a rope. Every Friesian horse has to have access to a salt lick in their shelter. That is the scope of your shelter or stall's furnishing.

Start Your Partnership Now!

As previously said, the goal of each interaction and activity you have with your Friesian horse is to strengthen your bond. With every interaction and activity, speak with your Friesian horse frequently. Share with him your opinions and remarks regarding each interaction. Give him a daily neck hug that lasts for at least 30 seconds. Smell him when you bury your face in his neck. Put your chest up against his. When you do this for the first time, he could be a little taken aback. The first few times, he could even try to move away from you. When he takes a step back, hold on. Join him as you move ahead and hang on for thirty seconds.

Your Friesian horse will quickly learn to appreciate your hugs as well. As you converse with him as needed, give him instructions. Say "Walk" as soon as you put on his halter and begin leading him out of his stall, and make sure he follows you out the door. Say "Stand" as you attach him to the hitching rail and praise him each time he follows instructions.

Appropriate Management

The most important thing to remember when handling your Friesian horse is to keep yourself safe. I'll say it again: if you don't know how to handle and ride a horse, you'll need to take some lessons before following along with these book instructions. You'll need to learn how to put on a halter, saddle and bridle, pick up each hoof and use a hoof pick to thoroughly clean the bottom of each hoof, and halter your Friesian horse so that he can lead out of the stall each day you work with him.

When handling a Friesian horse, you must be alert. If a dog runs up and starts your Friesian horse, he may react dangerously and try to run, kick, or even rear up in defence. If you are not alert and prepared, you could be dragged, kicked, or trampled. A Friesian horse can accidentally kill a human after being startled; to prevent this from happening, you may need to move out of the way or even release his lead rope to keep yourself safe. Regularly speaking to your Friesian horse in a soothing, calm voice will help prevent your horse from reacting as violently when he is startled.

Your Friesian horse will eventually become accustomed to a dog and become less frightened by most stimuli. However, if you have to walk past a herd of Llamas on a trail, he might get startled if he has never seen that kind of animal before. He might freeze, stare, and snort loudly with every breath out. Instead, calmly talk to him, stroke his neck, tell him they won't hurt him, tell him he's a good boy, squeeze his ribs with your legs to signal "Walk," and then walk past the herd of Llamas. After the third time, he probably won't react.

At first, it's beneficial to speak to your Friesian horse continuously, calming him through his worries. If you do this, your Friesian horse will face and conquer most of his fears rather fast.

Heavy Horse Breakdown

A horse must be broken before it can be trained. It's not as cruel as it sounds to break a horse. It merely indicates that the Horse is now able to follow instructions. It takes effort and perseverance to break a horse. When breaking a horse, there are various techniques and procedures to follow.

Forceful Breaking

It doesn't have to be difficult to break a horse. Some people think that the only way to break or train a horse is to mistreat it so badly that it becomes fearful of you and ultimately loses its soul. This is completely untrue because kindness and compassion may be used to train a horse.

Some trainers have adopted the mindset that building a rapport with a horse is time-consuming. If a horse exhibits uncooperative behaviour, it may be beaten without attempting to determine the underlying cause of the behaviour, such as fear or confusion. This relates to the notion that the Horse's spirit needs to be totally crushed to the point where it will obediently obey directions.

While leading a horse by power is necessary when training it, going too far might backfire. When a horse is broken in this way, fear alone may become its dominant motivation. When a horse is placed in an uncomfortable environment, it could start to fear its surroundings more than its instructor. The Horse may become uncontrollable as a result. A horse will learn to trust its teacher and become more at ease, even in stressful situations, if the trainer invests the necessary time and attention in training it.

There are alternative, less forceful ways to break a horse. The term "bucking bronco" refers to a method in which a wild horse is saddled and ridden until the animal gives up voluntarily. The possibility of damage to the Horse or the rider is a drawback of this strategy. For these reasons, using this procedure is not highly advised.

Horses can be incredibly devoted creatures. Many people think that handling horses requires harsh techniques, force, and even violence. It's the notion that a horse needs to be taught to respect that humans are superior to them. Even though this idea has mostly been abandoned, some people still try to train horses using these harsher techniques.

Appropriate Equines Training

Appropriate training of horses has numerous advantages. Making a horse safe to be around humans and useful for people to use is the aim of horse training. The most crucial element of teaching a horse is safety. A horse needs to learn social graces in order to keep people safe because it is far bigger and stronger than any person. By nature, horses are herd animals as well. This gives them the capacity to learn how to comply with and obey human directions. A horse that has received proper training will also learn to trust people. Horses must know when they may be secure in the company of humans since they have innate stress-reaction mechanisms. Beginning training your Horse at a young age is another piece of advice. Younger horses are more susceptible to influence and are better able to adjust to new environments.

Catching a horse is the first step in training it. You have to quietly approach the Horse and put it at ease. It should quickly be able to be led and made to move in the direction you desire once you have successfully attached a lead to its head. Leading the Horse around the pen, cleaning it, and generally providing for its needs will help the animal become accustomed to being handled by humans.

The Horse will be ready to wear a saddle in a few weeks. The Horse should be shown the saddle and should wear it several times. You can try mounting it in a few days. Mount the Horse with great care and patience. Try again if the Horse moves away. Of utmost importance is keeping the Horse tranquil.

Repetition is the key to properly training a horse. A horse needs to be properly cared for and ridden as much as possible. You may teach the Horse to trust and obey you if you give it enough time and loving attention.

Should the oedema not subside within a day, you can choose to schedule a stable appointment with your veterinarian. Even after losing one eye to blindness, some horses can still be ridden and function normally most of the time. Some horses go totally blind, but if there's no possibility of a stumble, they could be able to be ridden in mild terrain. That would only happen in a lifetime partnership between a really strong horse and rider. This book is actually meant to educate you on how to create, tend to, and grow that same kind of lifetime relationship.

The lifespan of a horse is 25 to 30 years. Some Horses survive into their forties and sometimes even older. In the 1800s, there was a horse that was reported to have lived for 62 years. A 56-year-old pony is said to have passed away in 2007. The relationship and affection you share with your Horse will only deepen with each passing year, even though the majority of it will blossom in the first year. I used to love to put my chest on my Horse's neck, rub my face against his, and embrace him at the base of his neck. I used to do this with him before I bought him to make sure he was a lovable horse with whom I could develop a bond.

Veterinary Exams for Your Equines

Before committing to a new horse, I will always get it checked out by a veterinarian. I usually won't get another checkup for another one to four years or until I start to notice any health issues. I want the veterinarian to weigh and examine his eyes, teeth, and hooves every time they visit. To maintain your Horse's health throughout its life, general care requirements must be met, in addition to enough nutrition and exercise. These consist of regular veterinarian care for teeth, feet, and immunisations; regular grooming and weatherproofing; and management of parasites. A reputable veterinarian will recommend foods and drugs for treatment. Elderly horses (those over 20 years of age) should see their veterinarian at least twice a year, if not more regularly, as sickness is more common and easier to diagnose in older animals.

Your Horse's doctor can suggest a wellness programme that includes frequent blood testing. I have owned my horses for ten years, and they are all over twenty years old. My closest friends treat my stables more like a retirement community! Right now, only one of the three can be ridden, but I want to give them the best possible life. These are happy horses living in a tiny heaven. They are fortunate.

Issues with Your Horse's Health

Although numerous things can happen even before the age of 20, the majority of health issues will manifest beyond that age. The majority of horses experience accidents or injuries before they experience health issues. Thoroughbred horses were injured in California in 35 per cent of all the races they competed in.

Because they exercise a lot, thoroughbred horses are more likely to experience lung haemorrhage.

Ten per cent or so have poor fertility.

5% of people have unusually tiny hearts.

Some have smaller hooves with thinner walls and soles, as well as less cartilage mass, which frequently causes foot pain and lameness.

Additional Horse Conditions:

Tetanus (Distemper) Strokes

Influenza

Equine encephalomyelitis and rhino pneumonitis

rabies

Worms in the stomach

Laminitis Colic

Sadly, there are a lot more health issues that can arise from accidents or injuries.

If you experience any symptoms, your veterinarian will also check for these illnesses. When a horse is suffering every day and has little possibility of rehabilitation, many horse owners will make the difficult decision to put their mount to death. Your Horse is incapable of making this choice on his own; it is a choice of Love. Sometimes, a veterinarian will tell you that you have a 10% chance of making a full recovery if you can afford to pay $5,000 or more for treatment and a hospital stay. Some horse owners don't have much money to throw away on a ten per cent chance. You might not have any health issues until the Horse is far into his 20s if you get one when he is 5-6 years old and in excellent health. It's typical to ride your Horse until he's over thirty years old or older.

You might decide to cover your Horse with a blanket on chilly evenings if you live somewhere where the temperature falls into the 20s and 30s. Considerations to make include if you would feel better about your Horse wearing a coat and whether he grows a particularly long winter coat. In either case, a nighttime blanket will help keep your Horse dry and toasty.

The winter water trough for your Horse is another thing to think about. A plug-in heater that may be placed in the trough for the winter is available at many stables. The water will never freeze if you use a plug-in heater. Your Horse will probably stick his nose through the ice to get water during the night if there is no electricity. If water is available during the freeze, you can remove the ice in the morning and replenish the trough. During the colder months, controlling the ice and flowing water can prove challenging.

Enhancing the Rhythm and Suppleness of Your Horse

Practicing rhythm

The three main gaits of a horse are walk, trot, and canter. The gaits are rhythmically repeated and even, and the trot and canter include a brief moment of suspension during which the Horse's four legs are off the ground. The regularity of each gait's steps is referred to as rhythm. The Horse's natural gait should be preserved while the steps have equal lengths and covers.

Regardless of speed, a horse's strides should be evenly spaced. The walk should have a distinct 4-beat pace and be vigorous but not rushed. The trot should have a distinct two-beat rhythm and move smoothly from one diagonal pair to the next. The canter should advance freely in an obvious 3-beat rhythm, covering the ground with steps, and then pause for a time. The Horse should actually go slightly slower than the speed at which he can keep his balance when he is moving in rhythm.

The Horse will pace more hurriedly and with shorter strides if you push him faster than he is comfortable with.

The young Horse will lose rhythm if the rider disturbs his natural balance once he has adjusted to the rider's weight. A horseback rider should sit gently, following the Horse's movements and not needlessly limit the Horse's forward motion with his hands.

The trot is the easiest tempo for a horse to keep time while being ridden; the canter and walk come next. Even though curved lines tend to keep a horse more relaxed, an excited horse benefits from a combination of exercises consisting of both straight and curved lines. Rhythm is typically best established on straight lines. Incorporate frequent rein changes and transitions to help your Horse become more adept at adjusting his balance so that he can move in time with you. Rhythm is emphasised highly in dressage exams because a horse can only use himself to the fullest extent possible if he can learn to maintain his rhythm, regardless of the task at hand.

Increasing Suppleness Even Further

When a horse is working freely through his back and is intellectually awake, his physical relaxation is typically described as looseness and suppleness, relaxation, and peace. Because the horse can then move freely, have flexible joints, work his muscles efficiently, and feel calmer mentally, this is regarded as a necessary condition for all training. A horse is nervous and rigid without them.

Look at the horse's general top line first to determine how supple he is. Is the horse's head held high and its back hollow, or is its neck stretching forward and its back lifting as the hind legs swing beneath the body? A happy, contented expression ("soft" eyes with typically no white showing around the edges and relaxed, not pinned back ears), a mouth that gently chews the bit with a little foam around the mouth (grinding teeth and excessive saliva running out of the mouth indicate stress and tension), a tail that moves with the rhythm of the gait and is not clamped in or swishing constantly, and soft, rhythmical breathing are other signs of looseness and mental relaxation.

Carry on with the supplying and balancing exercises you introduced earlier while you work with your horse to develop a rhythm. His flexibility and looseness, as well as his capacity to bend longitudinally (across his top line from head to tail) and laterally (from side to side), will all be enhanced by performing these gymnastic activities. With the help of this exercise regimen, you can help your horse grow, use all of his strength and work freely with a swinging back by encouraging him to engage all of his joints and muscles. His hocks, hips, knees, shoulders, poll, and jaw are the primary joints that you should supple and loosen. A block in the "flow" results from tension or stiffness in any one of these joints. You should ask your horse questions and provide aids, and he should take them gently. If your equine experiences anxiety during a particular activity and makes an effort to perform it, don't push through. Instead, switch to a less challenging exercise to help your horse regain confidence. Your horse will lose his composure and develop physical and psychological tension if you force him to perform workouts he is not ready for. Generally speaking, acknowledge your horse when he does an exercise well and disregard his unsuccessful attempts.

The introduction of increasingly challenging tasks is contingent upon your horse's training progress, individual aptitude, and confirmation. Certain conformation traits, such as a long neck and appropriate shoulder and hip angles, can influence a horse's inherent suppleness and facilitate the development of flexibility. Correct and consistent gymnastic activities may help your horse become less stiff or resistant, but if it persists, you should have your veterinarian look at it further.

A flexible equine freely moving through his back while extending his neck forward.

A stiff, hollow-backed horse with an overly elevated head. Not quite supple. He is not making good use of his back and hind legs.

When to Feed Your Horse an Andalusian

For horses to consume at least 20 pounds of hay every day, they must eat continuously. I've witnessed show horses being confined to stalls for up to 23 hours every day. In the winter, I've witnessed them being kept in the stall under heat lamps and blankets. They take this action to prevent the horse from developing a winter coat. In the world of show horses, a winter coat is not fashionable. We're thinking that if you owned a show horse, you would probably buy a training guidebook tailored specifically to show horses instead of this book.

The majority of people do not board horses in pastures without the need for regular feeding. Most Andalusian horses have two daily feedings—in the morning and the evening. You will allow your Andalusian horse to graze in the pasture for the majority of the day following the morning feeding. Your Andalusian horse will learn after a few days that the evening feed consists of grain and vitamins. When you call your Andalusian horse into his paddock to give him his preferred meal, he will anticipate it.

They adore grains and vitamins. It resembles a prize or a treat. They will soon pick up on the fact that you should yell his name or give a loud, sharp whistle. When you call him in, find a safe spot to stand since he might charge you at full speed. Although there is little chance that your Andalusian horse will run you over, it is safer to stand close to a fence post or other object that you are certain he won't run into for your safety.

You will eventually get enough confidence in your Andalusian horse to ensure that he never touches you or runs you down when entering their paddock.

Feeding your Andalusian horse twice a day allows for more time for interaction, training, and bonding. When you offer your Andalusian horse their favourite grain and vitamin combination, they will come to associate you with it. You will become his favourite human and will step up a notch if you feed your Andalusian horse twice a day (personally). If you are the one feeding him, this dynamic will probably happen sooner.

Being the herd's alpha leader and establishing your dominance are important aspects of horse management. For the time being, being an Alpha Status means you get to eat first; we explore this in our last chapter. Although it might appear insignificant, it plays a significant role in developing your alpha. You must wait patiently for your Andalusian horse to finish eating before he does. By doing this, you demonstrate your dominance and show your Andalusian Horse that you are in charge. Even before you call him in, he can be waiting in his paddock for feeding time. This is not going to happen every time the grass is in its active growing season. He might even have preferred the delectable fresh growth of grass to his food during that time. To begin training your Andalusian horse, you might need to go outside with him, put a halter on, and walk him to the paddock a few times. Probably the first few times, your Andalusian Horse will follow if he has a pasture companion who comes in immediately away.

Changing Foods

It can eventually become evident that, for a variety of reasons, switching to hay or grain is necessary. Use this switching schedule to swap out brands or types of food:

Day 1-2: Blend ¼ new and ¾ old food items.

Combine days 2–4 with day 1

Day 5–6: Combine ½ new and ¼ old.

Day 7: All new food, 100%

You should begin gradually, as mentioned above, while transferring your Andalusian horse from Alfalfa to Orchard Grass Hay, for example. It's a good idea to try your Andalusian horse on Orchard Grass or another grass hay if you find that he is becoming jacked up on lucerne due to its increased protein content. You'll probably notice that his behaviour has improved. You could choose to use "Mare Magic" on your Andalusian mare in order to balance her mood based on her cycles. Her behaviour will probably improve, and you will notice it. Mare Magic can likewise improve a Gelding's mood. If you see that your Andalusian horse has too much fat on his ribs, you may choose to cut back on his nutrition.

In order to help your Andalusian horse gain weight again, you can decide to add some rice bran to his diet after seeing that you can feel or see his ribs. It is customary to modify or alter your Andalusian horse's diet in order to preserve optimum health. It is advised that you get in touch with your veterinarian for further guidance if you are ever unsure.

Exams by a Vet for Your Gipsy Vanner Horse

Before committing to a new horse, I will always get it checked out by a veterinarian. I usually won't get another checkup for another one to four years or until I start to notice any health issues. I want the veterinarian to weigh and examine his eyes, teeth, and hooves every time they visit. To maintain your Gipsy Vanner Horse healthy for the duration of its life, additional general care requirements must be met in addition to adequate nutrition and exercise.

These consist of regular veterinarian care for teeth, feet, and immunisations; regular grooming and weatherproofing; and management of parasites. A reputable veterinarian will recommend foods and drugs for treatment. Elderly horses (those over 20 years of age) should see their veterinarian at least twice a year, if not more regularly, as sickness is more common and easier to diagnose in older animals.

For your Gipsy Vanner Horse, your veterinarian might suggest a wellness programme that includes regular blood testing. I have owned my horses for ten years, and they are all over twenty years old. My closest friends treat my stables more like a retirement community! Right now, only one of the three can be ridden, but I want to give them the best possible life. These horses, who reside in a small portion of paradise, are fortunate and content.

Issues with Your Gipsy Vanner Horse's Health

Although numerous things can happen even before the age of 20, the majority of health issues will manifest beyond that age. The majority of Gipsy Vanner Horses experience accidents or injuries before they experience health issues. Gipsy Vanner Horses are frequently affected by two conditions:

Persistently increasing lymphedema

Dermatitis of the pasterns

Additional Horse Conditions:

tetanus

Cushing's

Constriction (Distemper)

Influenza

Pneumonia in the nose

Encephalomyelitis in Horses

rabies

Worms in the stomach

Colic

Laminitis

Sadly, there are a lot more health issues that can arise from accidents or injuries.

If you experience any symptoms, your veterinarian will also check for these illnesses. When a Gipsy Vanner horse is suffering on a daily basis and has little chance of recovery, many owners will have to make the difficult decision to put their horse to sleep. It is not for your Gipsy Vanner Horse to decide; this is a choice of love. Sometimes, a veterinarian will tell you that you have a 10% chance of making a full recovery if you can afford to pay $5,000 or more for treatment and a hospital stay.

Some owners of Gipsy Vanner horses don't have a lot of money to throw around for a 10% chance. If you buy a very healthy 5–6-year-old Gipsy Vanner horse, you might not have any health issues until the horse is well into his 20s. It's common to ride your Gipsy Vanner horse until he's almost thirty years old or older.

You might choose to cover your Gipsy Vanner Horse with a blanket on chilly evenings if you live somewhere with lows in the 20s and 30s. Considerations to make include whether having your Gipsy Vanner Horse wear a coat will improve your mood and whether he grows a very long winter coat. In any case, a blanket will keep your Gipsy Vanner horse cosy and dry throughout the night.

The winter water trough for your Gipsy Vanner horse is another thing to think about. A plug-in heater that may be placed in the trough for the winter is available at many stables. The water will never freeze if you use a plug-in heater. Your Gipsy Vanner Horse will probably stick his nose through the ice to get water at night if there is no electricity. If water is available during the freeze, you can remove the ice in the morning and replenish the trough. During the colder months, controlling the ice and flowing water can prove challenging.

For example, your horse may develop anxiety when it crosses a tarp on the lawn. I wonder whether he was afraid he would trip, fall, or slip. For whatever reason, he refused to use the tarp as a walkway. This was resolved when he saw that another horse was led over the tarp and that the animal had not suffered any harm. His eyes showed surprise, and his ears sprang straight up. He never again felt afraid of it after that since he followed the other horse over the tarp. Make sure to repeatedly tell him, "good boy," whenever he conquers a fear. Let him understand that he won't be harmed by the things he fears. Assist him in forming constructive associations rather than destructive ones.

Your horse may develop timidity if he has a negative encounter with a person, another horse, or any other animal. However, if you take the time to help him overcome this fear and recondition him, it need not last forever.

It's a good idea to show him that not everyone is the Unabomber by exposing him to horses, other animals, and nice, joyful people. For obvious reasons, you should avoid someone who, while at the stables, yelled at your thoroughbred horse, for instance. Help him get over his phobia of people by exposing him to other calmer, more gentle individuals. A vital component of socialising your

Thoroughbred horse is helping him overcome his fear.

You might also want to show him other aspects of who you are. If you're an adult male with a beard, you can shave it off and wear a hat. In addition, if you so choose (I heard it grows back thicker). Instead of pants or jeans, you can wear a dress, shorts or sunglasses.

You can even switch up your hairstyle, shampoo, and aftershave by using a different scent. He'll be aware of these modifications. He will come to accept the fact that occasionally, your appearance or aroma changes if you keep talking to him and reassure him that everything is OK when you look different. He won't be as anxious about change after that.

Continue reading to learn how to look after your new best buddy.

When you first leave the stables, you might need to make a few shorter trips. You are less likely to encounter issues if you have been riding for a week or less after bringing your Andalusian horse to the stables. A condition known as "barn sour," which basically means that your Andalusian Horse is afraid to leave his safe stables for the big, scary rest of the world or wilderness, may cause you to notice more fear in your horse if you wait longer than a week.

The Andalusian horse is an animal of prey. They are inherently afraid of being eaten by bears or cougars, and they never know what to do if they see an elk or deer. Prepare yourself for your Andalusian horse's likely reaction if you encounter a strange creature while hiking. You could be in danger from this. Your Andalusian horse might attempt to toss you off his back or make a sudden high jump that will cause you to fall off. I'm just trying to get you ready, not to frighten you. Certain Andalusian horses will just stop and evaluate the circumstances. The most desired response is that one.

Gently turn your Andalusian horse away from the danger and walk him in that direction if he freezes and looks around. Keep him from backing away from a predator, not even at a trot. The bear or cougar will often follow the running instinctively. Keep your Andalusian horse at a trot; never run. Others will sprint off in the other direction, and you might find it hard to keep him under control. It might be necessary for you to leap off or just hold on for a few hundred yards or so.

As you are building a relationship with your Andalusian horse, there are a lot of challenges that you might encounter. You have to get ready ahead of time. He might turn out to be your true love. You ought to be aware of the risks and make preparations beforehand. When riding, we advise you to always wear a safety helmet. If you are riding a trail, we advise you to go with a second rider whenever feasible. You'll get out and move more as a result of this physical activity. Just stating.

Maintaining grooming

scrubbing

At minimum four times a week, you should brush your Andalusian horse's coat and clean his hooves. When an Andalusian horse is shedding in the spring, daily brushing is recommended. Before the warm summer arrives, he will have to lose his whole winter coat.

It's mutually soothing, I can guarantee you, before the long day starts.

One of the most healing and uplifting things you will do with your Andalusian horse is this. As much as you enjoy brushing him, he will adore being brushed. While you are brushing him, converse with him. Talk to him frequently using his name. Say "good boy" each time he stands up straight. Give the order, "Stand," if he starts to try to move away from you or around. Once he stops moving, praise him by saying, "Good Boy," and telling him to stop repeatedly. When they are young, some Andalusian horses may try to bite or kick you. NEVER ALLOW EITHER TO OCCUR! You must take precautions for your safety whenever you are around your Andalusian horse. Make sure he's not about to kick you by keeping a close eye on him. He might be considering it if he is standing with one leg bent back. If you never let him, he will never bite or kick you.

To ensure that he misses his kick if he attempts, you might want to give him some room while you move around him. You have to smack his nose away and tell him, "No biting," if he attempts to chew on your arm. You only need to backhand lightly. If you do hit your Andalusian horse, never hit it extremely hard. He will never consider biting or kicking you until he has fully bonded with you. If necessary, brush his entire body, neck, face, and legs. You'll clean every inch of his body, starting with the muck and working your way down to the dust.

Always keep oneself safe. Use a detangling brush to gently remove any tangles from his forelock and mane. Some tangles require cutting out because they are so severe. Once the mane is finished, do the same with his tail. Maybe you can stand right behind him and brush his tail in the future.

We advise you to start by standing to one side of his back and softly brushing his tail to one side. Keep in mind that you and your Andalusian horse may bond fast or slowly. It is excellent for everyone when selecting an Andalusian horse if he looks lovable to you PRIOR to purchase. That will guarantee that the bonding process happens considerably faster. The bonding process includes everything you do in the beginning with your Andalusian horse. You are building a lasting, healthy, and good relationship with your Andalusian horse, little by little. Please savour every moment while you go.

How To Take Charge Of Your Equine

Some attempt to lead their horse by using a lead rope to control the animal's head. The horse will draw back or push beyond the person holding the lead rope as a result of them pulling or jerking the lead rope. Since you don't want to tug or jerk your horse, there should be some leeway in the lead role as you guide him. You will halt the horse when he starts to go in the incorrect direction and force him to change direction with his body.

The key to properly maintaining control is mastery of your horse's physique. You can accomplish this by forcing him to turn his back on you in order to control his feet. One more term for this is disengaging the hindquarters. This is a great way to release tension and stiffness while virtually making your horse pay attention to you.

You can move your horse's hind end away from you in a few different ways. You can usually stand facing his shoulder and gesture to his hip.

Continue pointing and clucking at him if he remains still. If he doesn't move, click at him and tap him with the lead rope.

As soon as he moves, release the pressure on him. Don't forget to pat him and say, "Good Boy!" Next, request one more move. Then, you'll do it over again and request further action. You must keep in mind to perform this exercise on both sides of your body. You just need to point at his hip, and he will move them for you—it won't take long. To instil in him the idea that you are in charge, you will need to do this every day for a while.

Once you've moved him, grip onto your lead line and shift your body to walk forward. You'll detect a significant change. Your equine has directed his mind upon you. He's conscious of your movements and actions. To fix him if he makes a mistake due to distraction or fear, simply move his posterior once more. In little time at all, your horse will begin to sense your speed and will match your gait.

If your horse starts to gain ahead of you while you are leading him, move his hindquarters. If your horse starts to fall behind you, you will do this again. The movement of his hindquarters will be repeated each time he strays from your side.

The most fundamental training method is good control leading your horse. It's also how you get your horse into a trailer and move it around, wash it, and even ride it. These methods will teach your horse to be sensitive and gentle. You will have a horse that is sensitive and soft in the saddle if your horse is the same while you are mounted.

Section 13: Utilise Equine Education to Address Your Horse's Issue

It can be confusing to learn about equestrian training if you haven't studied it. A horse that exhibits behavioural issues is even more perplexing. The owner may become stressed and frustrated as a result. Many people are unaware that the trainer—rather than the horse—is typically the issue.

Analysing the behaviour of the horse is the first stage. For instance, a lot of riders have encountered scared horses. The horse's anxiety and fear that anything will "catch him" are shown by this. It's never a relaxing moment for the riders or the horses when they go for a ride.

Assuming that the rider is the reason for the horse's startle, we need to ascertain the rider's method. A novice horseman might not even be aware that he is tensely perched in the saddle. He might also have white knuckles from holding on to the reins and be as rigid as a plank. Horses are sensitive to these factors and will experience the same level of anxiety as a rider. This is a habit that horses can get into. Both the horse and the rider are scared by this since they are exacerbating each other's worries to the point where their anxiety will soar.

Due to his humanity and capacity for reason, the rider puts an end to the horse's illogical behaviour by stopping himself first. You need to unwind while seated. The horse will let you know when he notices a change if you are having fun and remaining relaxed. Then, you should speak with him to instil trust in him. Riding horses will become easier and more enjoyable as a result of the impending change in horse behaviour.

The rider merely uses riding to instruct the horse, whether they are aware of it or not. Never forget that you are training a horse every time you work with him. The encouragement the horse receives causes him to react. The horse will respond habitually if the encouragement is given on a regular basis. Stressful stimuli have the potential to evoke fear and produce a phantom horse.

This is but one instance of how your actions might influence a horse's behaviour. Although it's not entirely accurate, this is an excellent starting point for debugging. This is usually where the issue arises.

28 Sir Merger

10. What to Do If Your Ride Doesn't Go Right

For the past few rides, your horse has been excellent every time. He appears to have embraced the new regimen, and he's progressing so rapidly that you anticipate performing admirably in the upcoming season. Then it feels like you've regressed three steps all of a sudden. He's not reacting or listening the same way he did.

Everybody has bad days—me, you, and our horses included. Furthermore, pushing the matter might not be the best course of action. If your ride isn't going as planned, you may need to think about the following issues that could be the source of the unexpected behaviour:

Uncomfort: He might not be at ease. It's possible that he had a bad night's sleep and feels stiff now. Perhaps he was playing rough in the field with his friend, or perhaps he stumbled in his paddock and got a stone bruise. It's common to experience occasional headaches, stiffness, or sleeping on the wrong side of the bed. Perhaps he awoke on the incorrect side of his lavatory.

Illness: Severe malaise may indicate a medical condition, particularly a fever or even mild colic. He may not be feeling well and may be more susceptible to medical treatments if he recently received injections or dewormer.

Lameness: Lameness, particularly lameness in the hind legs, can be hard to diagnose. Run your hands over your horse's back and legs thoroughly to check for any lumps, heat, or discomfort.

New gear: It might not fit properly to use a new saddle orbit. Sensitive horses may become alarmed by anything as simple as a change in a bit, such as switching from a hunt seat to a western pleasure bit, or even just a change in saddle weight.

General weariness: Your horse may be weary, sore, and in need of some leisure if you've been really working with him every day.

The list could never end. Take into account the overall health and behaviour of your horse and rule out any disease, lameness, or pain. There are a few things you can do if your horse is simply having a rough day:

Reduce the intensity of the training. Forget about honing the more sophisticated skills you've been practising and instead on learning new things. Return to something simpler, something fundamental that he has long since mastered, and attempt to work at that level.

If he still doesn't seem like himself, you might choose to forgo the training entirely and use the time to go for a leisurely trail ride or low-key hack session. A horse may only require a change of scenery from time to time, particularly if he spends all of his time in the riding arena. He might be becoming irritable.

Take a stress-free ride with a pal. Sometimes, all it takes to de-stress both yourself and your horse is a riding partner and his horse.

Give it up for the day or a little while. Reduce the difficulty of the training to a minimum, give him a happy ending, and give him some time to himself to be a horse. Try riding him again later, or try the following day. It might only take him a couple of hours to go outside and graze on some grass.

Lastly, you should have been asking yourself whether there is anything you are doing to make your horse feel this way the entire time. Are you pressing him too rapidly or too hard? Is he too young to be expected to achieve this kind of progress? Are you allowing him time off so that he may rest and recharge? When he does something right, are you praising him, or are you pushing him harder and harder all the time? Is a wall separating you and your horse because of your drive and frustration?

It's possible to cut down on the number of days your horse isn't feeling quite himself if you take into account his needs, his learning style, and your relationship with him.

The Light/Forward Seat

Captain Caprilli gave the first demonstration of the Forward Seat in 1901 while he was in Italy. Italian cavalry commander and equestrian Captain Federico Caprilli invented the leaping seat. His stance, now referred to as the "forward seat," helped shape the contemporary jumping method that is currently employed by all riders.

The rider's seat is placed closely above the saddle in the forward seat but not inside of it.

With the head raised high and the shoulders not too far in front of the vertical, the rider's centre of gravity is above that of the horse.

The rider's weight is mostly transferred through the legs, with the heel being reached by flexible hips, knees, and ankles.

The calves and knees hold the saddle firmly.

The rider can clearly feel the stirrups since the stirrup leathers are cut short enough. The stirrup leathers in the forward seat are roughly three holes shorter than those in the dressage seat, but the best stirrup length for you in the forward seat will depend on your body type and flexibility, as well as the size and form of your horse.

Positioned somewhat behind the perimeter is the lower leg.

The ankle is gently curved outward and does not come into contact with the horse's side, and the heels are well pressed down.

The calf and knee approach the horse more because of the foot's small inclination, which guarantees a tight grasp and produces an independent, balanced seat during jumping.

Your foot rests on the inside of the stirrup, which lies beneath the ball of your foot.

Your calves' inner side is used to provide leg assistance. Avoid trying to use your ankles to squeeze your horse's sides, as this will force you to bend out your knees and calves, lose your solid stance, and be unable to provide independent rein aids in any situation.

Because the rider's upper body is positioned forward, the reins are held shorter than in the dressage seat. The hands are lifted off the equine's neck. Avoid riding with your fists open, and maintain your thumb and forefinger securely closed on the rein when gripping your reins.

To maintain a steady touch with the horse's mouth, you should have flexible shoulders, elbows, and wrists. Horses use their necks for balance, and you may help your horse stay balanced by maintaining a steady rein contact. Your horse's balance will suffer if you have very erratic rein touch. You cannot correctly control the 'front end' of your horse if you do not maintain continuous, positive rein contact. With loose or flapping reins, you cannot steer, flex your horse, or bend him around your inside leg. The same holds when riding your horse "on the bit" and producing impulsion. You can exert as much force as you like, but without a consistent, firm rein contact, all of the energy generated by your legs will exit via "the front door." The degree of interaction varies according to your horse (training level, conformation, etc.).

When riders wear stirrup leathers that are too long, they run the risk of losing their balance while jumping. This is because their lower leg may be in front of the perimeter, their toes may be pulled down, their heel may be pulled up, and their knees may not be gripping the ground properly. This can cause them to fall into the saddle, especially when they are jumping spread fences that may have hind leg faults on the back pole of the fence. They also force them to balance themselves with the reins, w

In addition to throwing off the rider's forward seat over a fence, too short stirrup leathers can cause the horse to swing backwards over the fence, causing the rider to support himself over the fence by resting his hands on the horse's neck. This can cause the horse to come on the forehand and possibly develop front leg faults.

Analysing The Information From The Interview

Even though each horse receives a net score based on the data, several factors should be discussed. Even if they might not do well on the T.R.A.I.L.S. assessment, young horses and quiet horses are still valuable. They can be excellent deals for less money if their flaws are not harmful. It's critical to identify the instances in which a horse does poorly because it is untrained and does not understand the question. For instance, a low overall score (below 50%) will be the consequence of low scores in numerous categories. For someone who enjoys a leisurely, quiet trail ride, a horse that exhibits sluggish behaviour may be quite calm and careful despite scoring poorly in certain categories. After the age of five, several outstanding horses have been produced. With the right amount of time and training, a quiet, intelligent horse can make an excellent trail horse. Conducting additional research is necessary before deciding to pursue a low-scoring horse. Should you choose to buy a horse with a low score, be ready to invest money and/or time to raise its level of performance. If this method had been in place when I bought one of my favourite horses, he would have been a poor scorer. Years later, he is still my ranch's top scorer and a beginner's babysitter. I was fortunate.

On the other hand, a lot of experienced riders should stay away from well-trained horses that lack enthusiasm. Even though these horses have high T.R.A.I.L.S. scores, they are too lazy and slow to meet your demands for play days or trail pace. Certain horses with high scores will make excellent followers rather than excellent trail-riding leaders. This is acceptable, and some riders even like these qualities, but as you start looking for your trail buddy, keep this in mind. It is frequently impossible to predict which horses will make good leaders and which ones won't. You can be let down if the horse you buy isn't bold enough to lead a trail ride. It is possible to teach many horses that are reluctant to lead at first by taking turns leading on trail rides, professional training, or trail riding alone. You can try to ride the horse during the interview, or you can ask the owner to ride it outside of the barn and see how they respond. If a riding interview isn't possible, you can just walk the horse away from the barn and gauge its comfort level. Although it can reveal a horse's degree of herd mentality, this is not a conclusive way to assess a horse's bravery. The majority of moderately to severely herd-bound horses are not good leaders. After you are comfortable with the scoring system, you can review the list and determine which criteria, given your riding competence, personality, and riding partner, are most or least relevant to you.

Here's another important thing to think about: Do you have the time, energy, will, and coordination to really get better at riding? Sincere introspection (self-evaluation) is never easy. Several indicators can assist you in figuring out what opportunities there are to get better at riding. You have varying chances of improving depending on your age, athleticism, fitness, body mass index (B.M.I.), amount of riding opportunities per week, and time since your previous ride. I won't rehash the point because I believe everyone is aware of where this is going. By all means, that horse is up for grabs if you envision yourself developing into a horse that is currently too spirited or hot for you. But for the more experienced trail rider, it is excellent advice to get the horse of your dreams now.

Cracked heel and mud fever

This skin ailment, which is characterised by skin irritation on the legs and stomach of afflicted horses, is brought on by muddy or wet environments. The scaly area can be irritated. Severe cases of mud fever can also cause fever or elevated temperature. The cause of mud fever is bacteria. Muddy or wet skin might allow bacteria to seep beneath the surface. Mud fever and cracked heels are related because the same circumstances cause them.

How to avoid and treat cracked heels and mud fever: anytime you bring your horse in from the field, you should wash its legs to avoid this illness. You have two options for removing the mud: either let it dry completely before brushing it off or just rinse the wet muck off with water and pat dry. Another option is to use a barrier lotion, which keeps the horse's skin from becoming too wet.

Delightful Itch

Sweet itch, sometimes called Summer Seasonal Recurrent Dermatitis (S.S.R.D.), is a kind of allergic reaction that causes skin irritation. It is common for the afflicted skin area to become itchy as well. The horse's back, mane, and tail are the most frequently impacted areas. It is brought on by a particular kind of midge known as Culicoides, sometimes known as "no-see-ums" or gnats, which irritates the skin and triggers an allergic response to its saliva. In severe situations, the horse could scrape itself raw on objects to relieve the itch.

A horse that develops this illness as a youngster will always have it, even though the condition's symptoms mostly rely on external factors.

Eliminating midges or grazing your horse away from midge-prone regions is the most reliable method of preventing sweet itch. Midges are drawn to places with a lot of decaying vegetation, which are usually found in forests or close to bodies of water. Steer clear of these areas. Midges are more prevalent at twilight or morning; therefore, avoiding grazing at certain times of the day can also assist in control and minimise contact with them.

Conditions Related to the Respiratory System

Typical Cold

A common cold in horses can cause a discharge from the nose that is white or yellow. Horses may also have enlarged nose glands and a mild temperature in addition to this. Contact with an infected person can quickly spread the viral virus known as the flu. Long-term storage of horses in stalls with inadequate ventilation increases the risk of infection. Your horses' proximity to other horses during shows may make them more susceptible to colds.

The best way to avoid or treat a common cold is to keep your horse apart from your other pets and contact a veterinarian right once. At all times, keep your horse in a well-ventilated location. Give diseased horses hay that is soft and easy to swallow (ideally wet). Restrict your horse's interactions with other horses at competitions and public displays, and try not to allow your horse to drink from public water troughs.

Cough

There are several causes of coughs. The most prevalent cough is typified by a watery discharge from the horse's nose and is usually connected to the common cold. This kind of cough can last for roughly two weeks, during which time it gets worse more often. Aside from bacteria and viruses, allergies are another common cause of coughing.

Coughs should be treated and managed as soon as possible. If your horse starts coughing, have them not work or engage in any other strenuous activity until they have seen a veterinarian. If a bacterial or viral illness is the reason, treat it. If your horse is coughing due to an allergic reaction, make sure that the area around them is clean and well-ventilated. Hay should be soaked in water to reduce dust, and bedding and other stable items should be clear of dust. Until the actual reason for the cough has been identified, it is always advised to keep the horse apart from other animals.

How to Desensitise Your Dog

Slowly and carefully begin stowing him down with an old, delicate seat material while holding the lead rope, for example, unrestricted. When foals get older, I usually hold the lead rope, which means your horse isn't restrained; it's just being held firmly by you to pack down. If it's feasible, try to pack down into a smaller yard so that you can easily move to the side of him if he pulls away.

The fluttering of the seat cloth on the foal is called "bagging down." Start with his front legs and work your way up and around his torso, using your entire body to flutter it.

He'll move, but maintain a firm lead to prevent him from getting around you. You must keep letting him go around you rather than letting him come back straight.

Instead of confronting him head-on and expecting him to retreat, move beside him and move out of the way. At that moment, turn his head to face you and keep slapping him around the shoulder until he stops. If he is still trying to pull back straight, move towards the hip to initiate the orbiting movement (don't sack him down; instead, use your hand and focus). Then, go back to packing down the shoulder area until he stops.

Continue without stopping, or otherwise, he will get afraid of the seat fabric, and you will be helping him to overcome his fear.

Continue moving cautiously even as he avoids you. Once he finally stops, assist for 30 seconds and then carry on sacking for another 10 seconds.

Change sides and repeat.

Removing the Halter

Remove the harness before releasing your colt back into the enclosure or yard with his mother. However, if you already do this, you don't need him to figure out how to back off. Securely wrap the lead rope around his neck and hold it near his head. After that, remove the strap and give his neck a gentle massage. At that moment, release the lead rope to let him proceed. By the third day, he should be standing even more subtly so that you can do this—of course, depending on his attitude.

Kitty is the name of my foal. She is incredibly perceptive and extremely nervous! Like her mother, actually!

After teaching her to release pressure, I briefly restrained her, and she withdrew. This obviously fixed the strap more than anticipated, so I was taking a little longer to unfasten the harness when it came time to release her.

She was becoming tense, stuttering and struggling. In this instance, I had to loosen the harness by pulling her towards me with the lead line around her neck with a somewhat abrupt and firm tug.

In the brief period of
During my "shock esteem" period, I managed to loosen the strap and remove it. Anyway, I kept her by the lead rope for a good ten seconds more and ran a hand over her neck to make sure she realised that it was faster and easier to just wait for her strap to be removed. She is still anxious, and I think it will

take her two or three months to lose some of that attitude. However, I would like not to break her spirit since, as I have stated previously, it is this mindset that will ultimately make her amazing.

After three days of being walked, driven, sacked, and given feet, your foal should be starting to understand. In addition to being much faster when standing to slow down, he should be an excellent driver, and I appreciate you holding his feet for about three seconds.

There is no compelling reason to do anything other than repeat these exercises three or more times each time you receive them. If you're working extremely hard, you should be able to break free from the cycle with less weight on both you and your foal.

Congratulate yourself once he is putting up with all of this preparation without any resistance. Congratulations! Your foal has learned to let go of pressure!

Awareness Is Required:

Horses are predisposed to be highly aware of anything that has changed or disappeared from their environment.

Since their eyes differ from ours, it's critical to be mindful of the following circumstances.

There is also a blind region under the horse's hind legs and his belly, depending on the form of his belly.

When we urge a horse to back over a rail, he is relying on recollection or feeling rather than his actual view of the rail at that moment. It doesn't follow that the horse can see it just because we can.

It is better to stay slightly off-centre when approaching the horse from the front to avoid being in his blind spot.

The horse's mind is not using his peripheral vision if he is fixating on anything in front of him in his field of view. This means that he may experience a startled reaction, sometimes known as "spooking," if something unexpected comes abruptly from behind him. The horse will want to turn and investigate the source of the spook, either by wheeling around or sprinting ahead; he will only turn when he feels safe enough to do so. Peripheral vision detects movement rather than detail.

In order to educate the horse to firmly maintain our visibility as we move left and right into and out of his blind spot, we must manoeuvre between his right and left peripheral vision while performing groundwork behind him. We can also train him to adjust his head.

Horses navigate jumps by jumping from their memory of the jump's location, which causes the jump to vanish from their field of view as they approach it. The horse will run straight into it without recognising its presence if he is focused on anything else as he approaches the jump.

Once we transition from groundwork to riding, the horse no longer recognises the familiar visual cues. We can facilitate the horse's transition from groundwork to riding by teaching pertinent touch and verbal cues.

After the horse is mounted, we must carefully teach him the new touch signals by first matching them with the verbal and visual cues he is already familiar with from his groundwork.

The transition to riding might simply be a part of a systematic evolution rather than a significant change if touch and verbal signals are clearly taught with first training.

2-2: Convening

We find it difficult to comprehend how much more hearing horses have than humans. If we employ words or sounds frequently, they quickly become signals. A horse may also learn to interpret sounds as environmental cues based on his routines while in captivity.

If the horse resides close to the handler's home, the house door opening

someone's vehicle pulling into the paddock (with a nice meal, goodies, or planned adventures)

tin can full of pellets or a pail of food

whistling to enter for a meal or reward

When we utilise Clicker Training, we fine-tune this response to sound by marking the exact response we seek with a click or other distinctive sound.

Equine ears possess ten distinct muscles that allow them to rotate nearly 180 degrees. The horse's ear structure enables it to hear more sounds farther away than human ears. Furthermore, horses have a greater and lower frequency range of hearing than humans.

Accurately determining the direction of sound is made possible by the structure and movement of the two ears. Sound and visuals are intertwined. Horses are prey animals in their ecology. Thus, they are wired to detect sounds, especially those that are uncommon or cunning.

Sounds elicit profound emotional reactions in horses. The loud noises and stressful atmosphere of exhibitions and events will be extremely exciting and troublesome for anxious horses. To help a horse become more accustomed to noisy, strange environments, it is helpful to gradually acclimatise them to this type of setting rather than relying on flooding (overstimulation until the horse "shuts down").

While grazing, horses appear to be able to detect vibrations from the ground through their feet, whiskers, and teeth. This undoubtedly has to do with the "early warning" that animals like horses and others can provide humans with regarding earthquakes and other calamities. That could also be the reason they are waiting for our automobile at the gate. However, that can also be a result of their hearing.

Four Little Stars

When Josie got back to the house, Aunt Sue was already up.

"Where have you been, Aunt Sue?" inquired.

Josie remarked, "I found the canyon trail and went down to the creek." Regarding the filly and the deceased horse, she had nothing to say. Not until she felt more confident about the future and how Aunt Sue would respond, anyway.

That's excellent, her aunt remarked. "Now that the land trust owns the canyon, not many people go along the creek, and not many people utilise that trail either. Thus, it's a fantastic location for some privacy.

Josie, thrilled to have this opportunity to find out more about land ownership, inquired, "What's the land trust?"

"Oh, they're a group that promotes environmental land preservation. They purchase land that they believe should be preserved. Then, they succeed in doing so. Keeping people and domestic animals off the land is a part of their management style. They even oppose you taking your dog for a walk there.

"You mean there's no longer use on the horse trails that Jack used to ride?"

No, sorry. The guides for the land trust may occasionally conduct a tour down there to showcase all the wonderful things they are doing to the public and media. The guided walks aid in their fund-raising efforts, as they are constantly in need of funds. Apart from that, the canyon is reverting to its natural state.

A couple of us who reside on the rim occasionally stroll down there. However, the majority of us are becoming older, and the ascent is gradual. Thus, not much is happening down there.

For now, that responded to the first query. The land trust did not own the dead mare or the filly. Josie would now have to inquire as to if anyone in the vicinity had lost a mare that was in foal.

That would be a lot harder question to ask, Josie thought. Aunt Sue would ponder the reason for her inquiry. Josie decided to postpone her queries for another day. She would need to try to get the filly to allow her to pet it first.

Aunt Sue said, "Okay, Josie." For the time being, living arrangements have been on my mind. Jack's room ought to be functional for you. You'll have access to the bathroom next door. It will be your responsibility to keep it tidy. We must get you additional clothing. You'll need more shirts, jeans, and shorts than you now own throughout the summer months here. Our fine dust makes things quite unclean. We should also get you a second pair of trainers. Today, we'll visit the city and make a trip to Bi-Mart. They will have all you require at this time.

"Are you able to cook?" asked Aunt Sue.

Josie remarked, "I can make soup and toast for supper." "I can also boil hot dogs," I'm skilled at using the microwave to reheat food. My mother used to say that I was incredibly self-sufficient.

"All of those are excellent options if you're low on food. However, Sam and I make an effort to eat healthful foods. It entails preparing meals from scratch. For example, preparing our salad dressing using high-quality vinegar, real olive oil, and spices. We have salads every day. Do you have a salad for supper?

Josie said in a quiet voice, "No." She never ate supper with a salad. That kind of food was expensive and often went bad before it was consumed, so Mom never kept it in the refrigerator.

"Alright, child," responded Aunt Sue. You will be learning a lot this summer. We'll take that self-sufficiency a step further and incorporate healthy self-sufficiency, just like your mother mentioned.

Josie stopped and considered Sam, her uncle. She recalled their first meeting day. "Please just call me Sam," he had pleaded. You already have a giant Uncle Sam because you're an American. His gentle demeanour and easy smile made him a pleasure to be around. He had blue eyes and blond hair, and he was powerful and athletic. She was comfortable with very few men, and Sam was one of them.

As they talked about roles and duties, Aunt Sue let Josie use her laptop as long as she turned it off when she was finished.

Josie was shown by Sue, who worked at the Sisters public library, how to place requests for books to be checked out and read. When Aunt Sue's requests from the library were complete, she promised to bring the books home.

This was one of the most important topics they had discussed, in Josie's opinion. Josie had never visited the public library with her mother. The school library had been made available for her to check out books, but it was tiny and contained only a small number of books about horses—the only subject Josie enjoyed reading about.

While Aunt Sue was teaching Josie how to look for books that she may request, the list of horse books appeared. There were a hundred books about horses, I think!

Josie realised that while she wasn't working with Little Star, she would have plenty of horse stories to read.

And that was it! She suddenly remembered the name. The filly's glossy brown forehead featured a little star in the centre. She would, therefore, refer to her as Little Star.

Never sit with your butt in the back of the saddle. When you ask your horse to rate a barrel, and you are front in the saddle, your horse will want to rate on his front end, which will push you forward and farther out of position for the turn. The rider's and the horse's equilibrium is lost when they lean forward in the saddle.

It is never appropriate to sit up and lean forward before your turn is over. Leaning forward too soon reduces your horse's ability to fire out of the turn and instead causes him to float out and bow off the barrel if he hasn't accomplished his turn.

Never lean and shift your weight from one stirrup to the other. Your horse will have to adjust by dropping his opposing shoulder in order to accommodate the change in your weight. You can cause your horse to become unbalanced and out of position during a turn by shifting your weight to one stirrup. Additionally, it overly strains the horse's withers and may cause your saddle to misalign the horse's spine.

Never adjust your saddle by shifting your body weight. Avoid attempting to roll your saddle back by placing all of your weight in one stirrup and stepping on it if it rolls to one side. This may force your horse's spine out of alignment, resulting in excruciating discomfort and injury.

BREL PATTERN

The barrel pattern for the American Quarter Horse Association (AQHA) is typically 45 feet long, spanning from the gate to the timer line; from the timer to the centre of the first and second barrels, it is 60 feet long; between the first and second barrels, it is 90 feet; between the second and third barrels, it is 105 feet long; and finally, it is roughly 145 feet long, spanning from the third barrel to the timer line. With all of the angles, the overall distance is about 495 feet from the timer line through the pattern, around the barrels and back to the timer line.

A barrel pattern is always measured from the inside of the arena, not from the end of the alley, even though some arenas feature an alley for entry. Although side or offset entry gates are still present in some venues, centre entry gates remain the norm.

An electronic eye times the majority of barrel races held nowadays. Hand timing is simply not precise enough, with the difference between first and second place being only hundreds and thousands of seconds.

The actual distance that the horse must travel on an AQHA pattern when done correctly, comes to a total of about 495 feet when broken down. From the timer line, there are 65 feet to the first barrel, 30 feet to the first barrel's circumference, 90 feet to the second barrel's circumference, 105 feet to the third barrel's circumference, and a final 145 feet back to the timer line.

In today's sport, you must finish these 495 feet on a regular AQHA barrel pattern in around 17.00 seconds to guarantee a cheque at a barrel race. This means that in a typical barrel pattern, your horse's every three feet is worth almost a tenth of a second.

Not every arena has the space to set up an ACHA pattern (standard Quarter Horse

Association). The pattern must be adjusted for smaller venues to meet the venue's dimensions. This results in a quick time off, depending on the size of these smaller designs, anywhere from 12 seconds and higher. With the smaller patterns, we lose much more time per foot—more than a tenth of a second—which means we have even less tolerance for error when running on them.

We're going to disassemble these 495 feet in this book and figure out just where we have to run in our cloverleaf pattern in order to finish it in 17 seconds.

www.ingramcontent.com/pod-product-compliance
Lightning Source LLC
Chambersburg PA
CBHW052146110526
44591CB00012B/1880